WOMEN'S PRO BASKETBALL TODAY

THE HISTORY OF THE CLEVELAND

ROCKERS

JOHN NICHOLS

Published by Creative Education
123 South Broad Street, Mankato, Minnesota 56001
Creative Education is an imprint of The Creative Company

Design by Stephanie Blumenthal
Cover design by Kathy Petelinsek
Production design by Andy Rustad

Photos by: NBA Photos

Library of Congress Cataloging-in-Publication Data

Nichols, John, 1966-
The History of the Cleveland Rockers / by John Nichols.
p. cm. — (Women's Pro Basketball Today)
Summary: Describes the history of the Cleveland Rockers professional women's basketball team
and profiles some of their leading players.
ISBN 1-58341-009-0

1. Cleveland Rockers (Basketball team)—Juvenile literature. 2. Basketball for women—United States
Juvenile literature. [1. Cleveland Rockers (Basketball team).
2. Women basketball players. 3. Basketball players. I. Title. II. Series.

GV885.52.C58N53 1999   99-18892
796.323'64'0977132—dc21   CIP

First Edition

2 4 6 8 9 7 5 3 1

As the ball bounces high off the side of the rim, the Cleveland Rockers' fast break is set into motion. The rebound is seized by the strong hands of Rockers center Isabelle Fijalkowski, who alertly fires a bullet outlet pass to a streaking Suzie McConnell Serio. The lightning-quick point guard kicks it into overdrive, speeding away from the slower defenders. At the free throw line, McConnell Serio looks to her left while deftly zipping a pass behind her back to the right. At the receiving end of the pass is hard-charging guard Michelle Edwards, who powers her way through a sea of upraised hands to lay the ball off the glass and into the basket. The fans at Gund Arena rise to their feet as one and explode into wild cheers. This is Cleveland Rockers basketball at its finest.

SUZIE MCCONNELL SERIO

PLAYS A KEY ROLE IN

CLEVELAND'S SUCCESS.

CLEVELAND—A CITY THAT ROCKS

The city of Cleveland is situated in the northeastern corner of Ohio. Bordered on the north by one of America's Great Lakes, Lake Erie, Cleveland has long been a city that has made its living on the water. For generations, the raw materials used to build America have traveled through Cleveland's port. Iron ore from Minnesota, grain from Iowa, coal from West Virginia—all flow to and from Cleveland's shores on a daily basis.

Another of the city's claims to fame is one of America's favorite tourist attractions: the Rock and Roll Hall of Fame and Museum, situated in Cleveland's downtown. All of the greatest rock legends—from the Beatles to the Who—have been inducted into the beautiful structure.

Cleveland is also known as a town that loves its sports. The Cleveland Indians of the Major League Baseball Association were established in 1901 and have grown into the very fabric of the city. Despite decades of losing seasons, the community's loyal fans continued to cheer for their team. Today, under new ownership, the Indians are one of the game's most stable and successful franchises.

The city's beloved Cleveland Browns of the National Football League, who moved to Baltimore in 1996 and became the Ravens, have returned to Ohio as an expansion franchise to begin

MICHELLE EDWARDS (ABOVE); GUND ARENA, HOME OF THE ROCKERS (BELOW)

FORWARD EVA NEMCOVA HAS NEVER MISSED A START.

play in 1999. The Cleveland Cavaliers of the National Basketball Association survived a shaky start in the early 1970s and today can count itself among the NBA's finest teams.

On October 30, 1996, Cleveland fans cheered the arrival of a new team when the WNBA, the Women's National Basketball Association, announced that Cleveland would be a charter member of the new eight-team league. "It's an exciting day for the city," proclaimed Cleveland mayor Michael White. "The WNBA is a perfect fit in Cleveland, and we are thrilled to be a part of it."

Cleveland's WNBA team would have the same stable ownership under brothers Gordon and George Gund that transformed the Cavaliers from NBA doormats to contenders. The team—which would play in Gund Arena—would be known as the Rockers, in honor of the Rock and Roll Hall of Fame.

WNBA president Val Ackerman announced that the league would begin its 28-game season in June 1997, shortly after the NBA season wrapped up. The new league soon coined a phrase to announce that pro basketball excitement didn't end with the NBA Finals. "We Got Next" became the rallying cry of a new league whose time had come.

HILL-MACDONALD BUILDS A WINNER

One of the toughest jobs for a professional coach is to build a team from scratch. Bringing in the right players and getting them to play as a team can be an unforgiving task—one that ends many coaching careers before they start. For Linda Hill-MacDonald, however, the challenge of coaching the Cleveland Rockers

was irresistible. "All my life I've dreamed of the day when women's pro basketball would be a reality in the U.S.," Hill-MacDonald said. "When I was offered this job, my dream came true."

Prior to joining the Rockers in May 1997, Hill-MacDonald had coached for 17 years in the college ranks. Before her arrival as a young coach at Temple University, the Owls had posted just one winning season in seven years. With Hill-MacDonald at the helm, though, the Owls posted seven winning seasons in 10 years, and Hill-MacDonald captured Atlantic 10 Conference Coach of the Year honors in 1987 and 1989. Hill-MacDonald later moved on to the University of Minnesota, where she led the Gophers to some of their best seasons ever.

Rockers president and general manager Wayne Embry pointed to Hill-MacDonald's proven ability to evaluate talent and build teams from the ground up as the deciding factors in her hiring. "Linda's energy and commitment to winning made her an obvious choice," he said. "She always gets the most out of her players."

Hill-MacDonald's brand of basketball demands that her players be unselfish and disciplined. Rugged defense and precise half-court offense are the hallmarks of her coaching style. "I love to get out and run, but to win close games, you have to execute your set plays," she said. "In a league where the talent is pretty equal, if you can execute better than the other team, you'll win."

TALENTED FORWARD

RUSHIA BROWN (ABOVE);

TANJA KOSTIC (LEFT)

DURABLE ROCKER FORWARD JANICE BRAXTON

Still, creating a cohesive team in a little more than a month out of a group of players coming from all parts of the world would be the challenge of a lifetime. "There were days early on when the pace was overwhelming," admitted the Rockers coach. "But the opportunity to work with players of this caliber has been rewarding on every level."

EDWARDS AND BRAXTON STEADY THE ROCKERS

Every good team needs players that can be counted on for consistent effort night after night. In a long professional season in which extensive travel is the rule and there is little time for rest, there are nights when players' energy levels wane. It is at such times that a good team's seasoned veterans lead the way to hard-earned victories.

For the Cleveland Rockers, the two players who would form the team's backbone were guard Michelle Edwards and forward Janice Braxton. "Michelle and Janice have been through the wars, and they take pride in being professional," said general manager Wayne Embry. "They always give you everything they have."

Edwards and Braxton were the first two Rockers in the history of the franchise, as both were assigned to Cleveland before the 1997 season. The WNBA wanted to make sure that each franchise had two solid veterans to build around, and Edwards and Braxton fit the bill nicely.

JENNY BOUCEK EARNED A

ROSTER SPOT THROUGH

TRYOUTS (ABOVE);

RAEGAN SCOTT (BELOW)

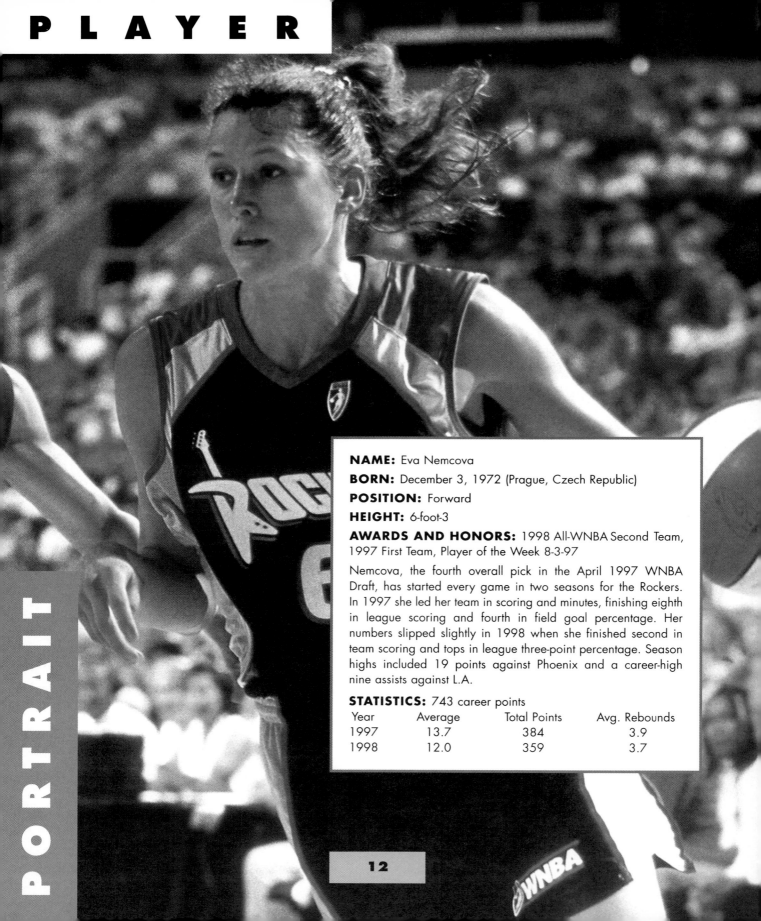

NAME: Eva Nemcova

BORN: December 3, 1972 (Prague, Czech Republic)

POSITION: Forward

HEIGHT: 6-foot-3

AWARDS AND HONORS: 1998 All-WNBA Second Team, 1997 First Team, Player of the Week 8-3-97

Nemcova, the fourth overall pick in the April 1997 WNBA Draft, has started every game in two seasons for the Rockers. In 1997 she led her team in scoring and minutes, finishing eighth in league scoring and fourth in field goal percentage. Her numbers slipped slightly in 1998 when she finished second in team scoring and tops in league three-point percentage. Season highs included 19 points against Phoenix and a career-high nine assists against L.A.

STATISTICS: 743 career points

Year	Average	Total Points	Avg. Rebounds
1997	13.7	384	3.9
1998	12.0	359	3.7

NAME: Isabelle Fijalkowski

BORN: May 23, 1972 (Clermont Ferrand, France)

POSITION: Center

HEIGHT: 6-foot-5

COLLEGE: Colorado '95

The second pick in the '97 Elite Draft, Fijalkowski led the Rockers in field goal percentage and finished second in scoring in 1997. Her numbers increased the following season when she led her teammates in scoring, field goal percentage, and rebounds. In 28 games, she scored in double digits 20 times and led the team in rebounding 17 times. Her .547 field goal percentage was best in the WNBA. In Cleveland's playoff series against Phoenix, she twice led the Rockers in scoring and rebounds.

STATISTICS: 715 career points

Year	Average	Total Points	Avg. Rebounds
1997	11.9	332	5.6
1998	13.7	383	6.9

PORTRAIT

13

In the Rockers' inaugural campaign, the experienced tandem combined for 22 points, 11 rebounds, and three assists per game. In 1998, surrounded by more talent, they would combine for 18 points, eight rebounds, and three assists per night. The fierce attitude of both players shines through in the advice Braxton gives to young people. "If you're going to do something, do it well," she said. "Do it all out or do nothing."

Edwards and Braxton brought a combined 19 years of European professional experience to the Rockers. The 5-foot-9 Edwards, known as "Ice" to her teammates for her on-court cool, played college ball at Iowa and was the first female Hawkeye to ever have her number retired. The Massachusetts native gives the Rockers silky-smooth guard play and a tough defensive presence.

The 6-foot-3 Braxton attended Louisiana Tech University, where she led the Lady Bulldogs to two NCAA championships in 1981 and '82. Her size and tenacity make her a true force to be reckoned with at the power forward position. "Braxton is a warhorse," declared Phoenix head coach Cheryl Miller after the big forward poured in 21 points against the Mercury. "She played in college back when I did, but she's still able to take over a game."

5-FOOT-9 GUARD MICHELLE EDWARDS

Due to their years of playing overseas, both Braxton and Edwards speak fluent Italian, but for the Rockers, the veteran duo communicate best in the most universal language of all: winning.

EVA AND "ISA" BRING WORLDWIDE APPEAL

When Rockers fans brag that their team features some of the world's best players, they're telling the truth. In forward Eva Nemcova and center Isabelle Fijalkowski, the Rockers have two foreign-born stars who have taken the WNBA by storm.

The 6-foot-3 Nemcova was born and raised in the Czech Republic. Her parents were both Olympic athletes, and Nemcova showed early on that she had the makings of a great athlete as well. By the age of 20, the agile forward had already played professionally for two years and had represented her country in the 1992 Olympic Games in Barcelona, Spain.

"Eva is so versatile," Embry said of the young star. "She runs well, she can handle the ball, and she can shoot the lights out. When we heard she was interested in coming over to the states to play, we crossed our fingers that she would be available when our pick came."

Embry's wish came true when the Rockers selected Nemcova with the fourth overall pick in the 1997 draft. The six-year

TANJA KOSTIC (ABOVE);

RESERVE FORWARD

RAEGAN SCOTT (BELOW)

veteran of professional European basketball immediately gave the Rockers a proven weapon to take into battle. "When we began camp, we were all waiting to see how good she was," Hill-MacDonald recalled. "Eva didn't disappoint."

The multitalented forward helped the Rockers on all fronts during their first season, leading the team in scoring eight times and assists twice and averaging 3.9 rebounds a game for the season. Nemcova's 13.7 points-per-game average ranked her eighth among the league's leading scorers in 1997. She also earned a reputation as an expert marksman, burying a league-high 44 percent of her shots from outside the three-point arc. For her efforts in 1997, Nemcova earned First-Team All-WNBA honors.

Teaming up with Nemcova along the Rockers' front line was the 6-foot-5 Fijalkowski. The French-born center had come to the United States in 1994 after a brilliant amateur career with the French National Team. She played one season at the University of Colorado before returning to Europe to play in the professional leagues. Two years later, Fijalkowski returned to the U.S. to play in the WNBA.

ANITA MAXWELL WAS

WAIVED IN MAY 1998

(ABOVE); ISABELLE

FIJALKOWSKI (BELOW)

From the moment she walked on the court, "Isa"—as she is known to her teammates—commanded respect. "Fijalkowski is strong, but she can beat you so many ways," Houston Comets coach Van Chancellor explained. "She's tough on the low block, but she also passes as well as any center in the league." The 25-year-old center averaged 11.9 points, 5.6 rebounds, and 2.4 assists a game in 1997 in a tremendous showing of her all-around game.

With their two talented imports leading the way, the Rockers would roll to a winning first season. The team rebounded from a 3–8 start to win a league-high eight straight games in the WNBA's first season. The Rockers finished 1997 with a 15–13 record, tied with the Charlotte Sting for the final spot in the playoffs. Due to Charlotte's better record in the Eastern Conference, however, the Sting were awarded the playoff berth. "It was tough to take," sighed guard Merlakia Jones. "We battled so hard to get back in it, but the early losses caught up to us."

MCCONNELL SERIO RUNS THE SHOW

With the 1998 draft fast approaching, Embry and Hill-MacDonald knew that their team needed one ingredient to change it from a good team to a great one—leadership. "We considered a lot of fantastic players, but one in particular kept coming up in our conversations," Hill-MacDonald said. "We kept talking about Suzie McConnell Serio, but then we'd shrug our shoulders and say, 'Nah, she's been out of the game too long.' But we couldn't get the idea out of our head."

The 5-foot-5 McConnell Serio had been a star guard for Penn State University from 1985 to 1988. Known for her quickness and exceptional ball-handling skills, McConnell Serio averaged 14.9 points and 10.2 assists over the course of her college career. Also an amazing passer, McConnell Serio set the NCAA record for assists in a career with 1,307.

After college, the Pennsylvania native led the U.S. Olympic team to gold in the 1988 Games in Seoul, Korea. Following the Games, McConnell Serio turned down many lucrative offers to play professionally overseas. She decided instead to stay close to home as head coach of the girls basketball team at Oakland Catholic High School in Pittsburgh.

In 1992, the fiery point guard laced up her sneakers once again to lead the U.S. Olympic team to another medal, this time a bronze in the 1992 Games in Spain. But from 1993 to 1997, she stayed on the bench, coaching Oakland High to a Pennsylvania state championship while enjoying family life with her husband and four young children. "We thought it was a long shot at best that Suzie would even entertain the idea of making a comeback at 32 with all the things she had going on in her life," Hill-MacDonald said.

Still, the hopeful Rockers did their best to lure McConnell Serio back to the court. After giving it a lot of thought, McConnell Serio decided that the WNBA was an opportunity she could not pass up. "I needed a perfect situation in order to consider it," McConnell Serio explained. "Cleveland is close to home, and the WNBA's summer season doesn't interfere with school or coaching. I couldn't resist."

After taking the point guard in the second round of the draft, Cleveland knew that it had its leader. McConnell Serio's imaginative passing, competitive nature, and coach-on-the-floor smarts boosted the Rockers to a new level. In her first game as a player in six years, McConnell Serio netted 10 points, dished out 10 assists, and had three steals in a 78–71 Rockers' victory over the New York Liberty. The 32-year-old played 38 of the game's 40 minutes, and the 17,911 fans in attendance at Gund Arena were on their feet at the game's end. "Wow, that was something, wasn't it?" asked a smiling Hill-MacDonald. "What a treat for our home crowd."

GUARD CINDY BLODGETT

WAS THE SIXTH PICK IN

THE 1998 WNBA DRAFT.

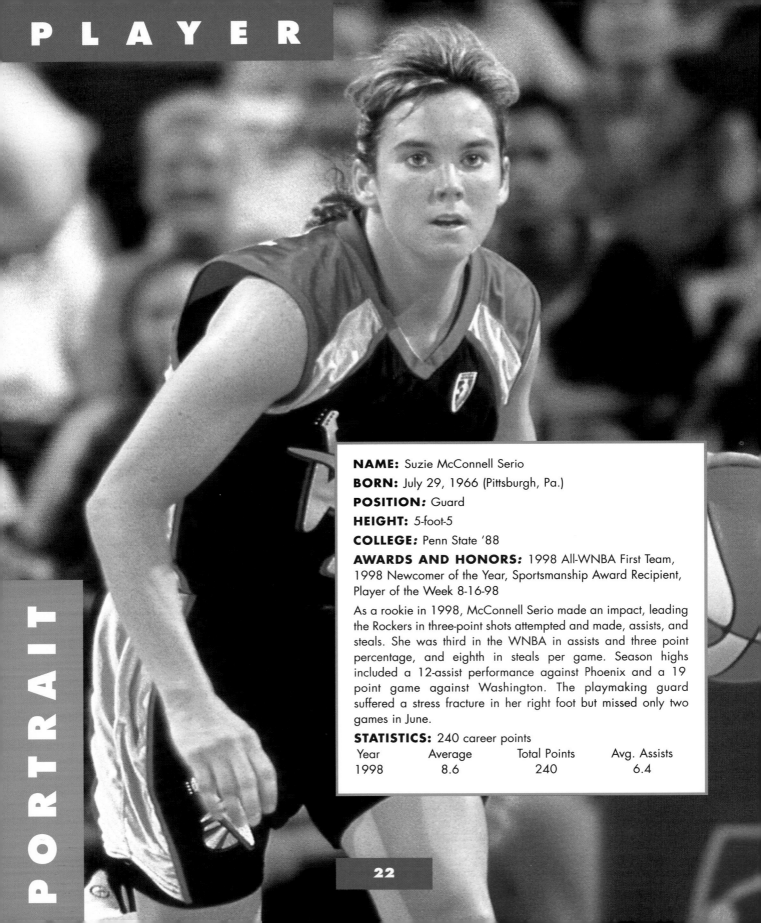

NAME: Suzie McConnell Serio

BORN: July 29, 1966 (Pittsburgh, Pa.)

POSITION: Guard

HEIGHT: 5-foot-5

COLLEGE: Penn State '88

AWARDS AND HONORS: 1998 All-WNBA First Team, 1998 Newcomer of the Year, Sportsmanship Award Recipient, Player of the Week 8-16-98

As a rookie in 1998, McConnell Serio made an impact, leading the Rockers in three-point shots attempted and made, assists, and steals. She was third in the WNBA in assists and three point percentage, and eighth in steals per game. Season highs included a 12-assist performance against Phoenix and a 19 point game against Washington. The playmaking guard suffered a stress fracture in her right foot but missed only two games in June.

STATISTICS: 240 career points

Year	Average	Total Points	Avg. Assists
1998	8.6	240	6.4

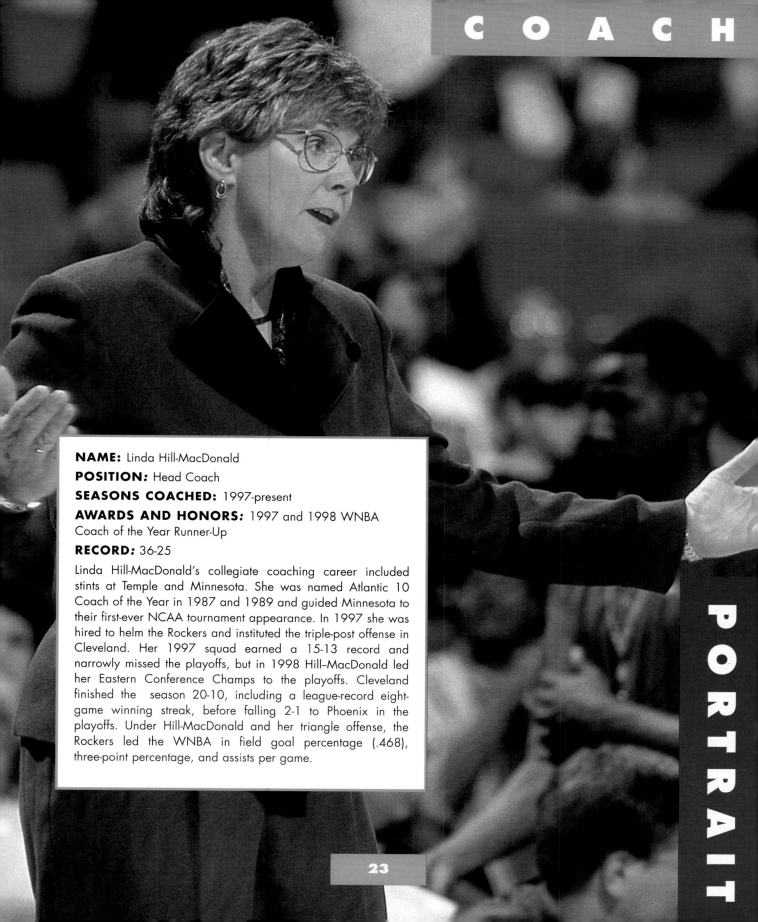

NAME: Linda Hill-MacDonald

POSITION: Head Coach

SEASONS COACHED: 1997-present

AWARDS AND HONORS: 1997 and 1998 WNBA Coach of the Year Runner-Up

RECORD: 36-25

Linda Hill-MacDonald's collegiate coaching career included stints at Temple and Minnesota. She was named Atlantic 10 Coach of the Year in 1987 and 1989 and guided Minnesota to their first-ever NCAA tournament appearance. In 1997 she was hired to helm the Rockers and instituted the triple-post offense in Cleveland. Her 1997 squad earned a 15-13 record and narrowly missed the playoffs, but in 1998 Hill–MacDonald led her Eastern Conference Champs to the playoffs. Cleveland finished the season 20-10, including a league-record eight-game winning streak, before falling 2-1 to Phoenix in the playoffs. Under Hill-MacDonald and her triangle offense, the Rockers led the WNBA in field goal percentage (.468), three-point percentage, and assists per game.

PORTRAIT

The Rockers' new sparkplug would continue to treat Cleveland fans to great performances as the team bolted to a 4–1 start. McConnell Serio proved her toughness and dedication to the team by returning to the lineup just one week after suffering a stress fracture in her right foot. "She sets an example for everybody," forward Janice Braxton summed up.

McConnell Serio also set a standard for the league, averaging 8.6 points, 6.4 assists, and 1.8 steals a game. For her steady play, she would go on to be named the WNBA Newcomer of the Year and an All-WNBA First Team selection at the end of the 1998 season.

Still stinging from their narrow miss of the 1997 playoffs, the Rockers showed grim determination as they fought their way to the 1998 postseason. The WNBA season had expanded to 30 games in the league's second season, and Cleveland treated each contest as a do-or-die situation. "We knew what it was like to come up short," guard Merlakia Jones pointed out. "We didn't want that to happen again."

Despite the team's focus, Cleveland's record stood at 12–9 at the end of July, and its playoff hopes looked bleak. With the season in jeopardy, the team regrouped and targeted the month of August for a stretch run. Up first that month would be a road game against the defending WNBA champions, the Houston Comets, and their star, Cynthia Cooper. The Comets had dominated the league, running up an amazing 20–1 record prior to the August 1 contest. The Rockers knew that they needed the win to prove that they were a playoff-caliber team.

After surging to a 40–29 halftime lead, the Rockers stumbled under intense pressure from the rallying Comets. With 7:40 left in regulation, the Comets clawed their way to a 57–56 lead, and suddenly it was gut-check time for the Rockers. "It was a big moment in the season," Hill-MacDonald admitted. "We could have folded up right there, but instead, we stepped it up a notch."

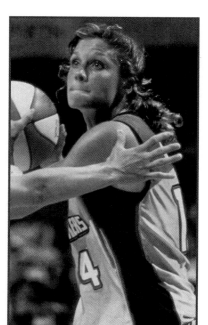

The teams traded baskets down the stretch, and the score stood at 68–68 at the end of regulation. In overtime, Merlakia Jones was outstanding, scoring four points in the final 34 seconds to boost Cleveland to a thrilling

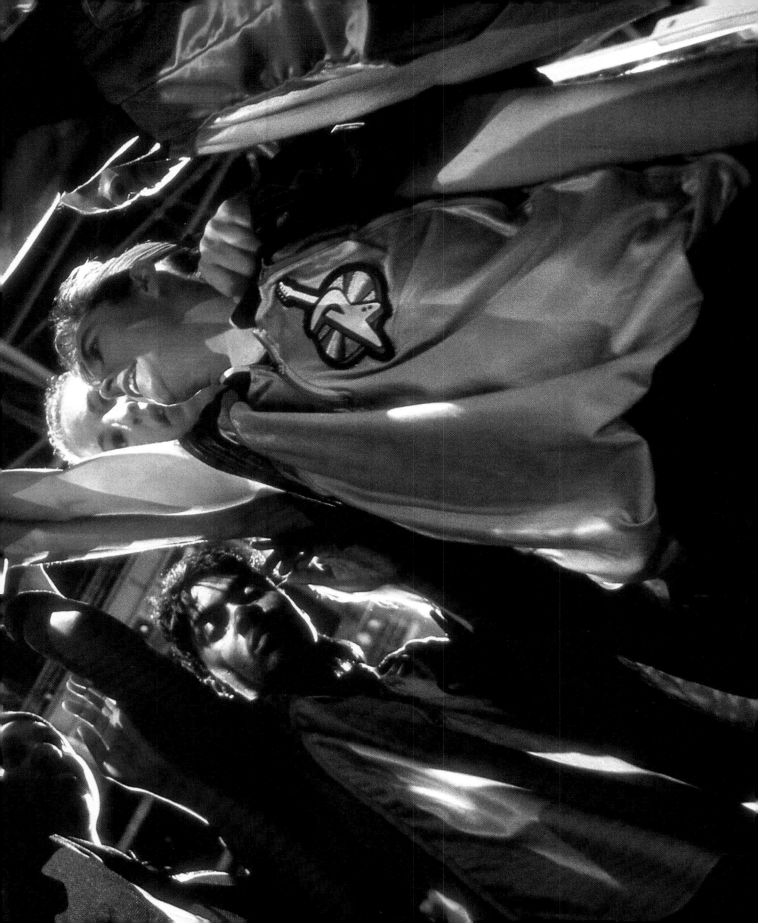

74–71 victory. "That win set the tone for the rest of the season for us," said Michelle Edwards. "After beating Houston, we knew we could beat anybody."

The confident Rockers went on a tear for the remainder of the regular season, winning six of their next seven games by an average of 12 points. The month-long rampage pushed the Rockers into first place in the East with a 19–10 record and set up a showdown with the New York Liberty for the conference title. The 18–11 Liberty, led by stars Rebecca Lobo and Teresa Weatherspoon, trailed the Rockers by just one game and would be playing on their home floor in front of 17,396 screaming fans. "It was a tough situation," remembered Fijalkowski. "They needed the win to make the playoffs, and we knew they would come out determined."

With New York's Madison Square Garden rumbling with noise, the undaunted Rockers came out and took care of business. Sparked by a monster effort from Fijalkowski, who scored 18 points and grabbed nine rebounds, the Rockers scratched out a hard-fought 70–64 win over the Liberty. With their 20th win of the season, Cleveland clinched the Eastern Conference championship and the second seed in the WNBA playoffs. "What a gutsy win," exclaimed an exuberant Coach Hill-MacDonald after the game. "The city of Cleveland has a lot to be proud of."

MICHELLE EDWARDS

(ABOVE); CLEVELAND

EARNED A PLAYOFF

BID IN 1998 (BELOW).

POSTSEASON IN CLEVELAND

After clinching the Eastern Conference championship, Cleveland ventured happily into unknown territory: the WNBA playoffs. With the top four teams advancing, the second-seeded Rockers drew the third-seeded Phoenix Mercury in the first round.

The matchup would be a tough one for the Rockers, who had dropped five of six regular-season contests to the small but speedy Mercury. "If we can slow the pace of the game down and pound it inside, we should be all right," Braxton said. "If it's a track meet, we'll have problems."

The three-game series would begin at Phoenix's America West Arena, and the Mercury would guard their home turf with gusto, winning 78–68. The Rockers were led by their big center, Isabelle Fijalkowski, who dropped in 20 points and grabbed nine rebounds, but the Mercury's Jennifer Gillom countered with 21 points of her own to lead Phoenix to the win.

In game two, the series moved to Gund Arena, where Cleveland slowed the fast-breaking Mercury to capture a 67–66 victory. Michelle Edwards rose to the occasion, tossing in 18 points, while Janice Braxton pounded the boards for 10 rebounds. "The crowd really got us pumped up, and we got the job done," said McConnell Serio,

ADRIENNE JOHNSON

(ABOVE); GUARD

CINDY BLODGETT

(BELOW)

who dished out nine assists in the victory. "It was a heck of a game, and it sure felt good to get that first playoff win."

Both teams had won on their respective home floors by dictating the tempo of the game. The third and deciding contest would be no different. It was a classic battle—speed versus power—and this time speed won out. The faster Mercury overcame a 35–32 halftime deficit and surged to a 71–60 victory at Gund Arena. "We got off to a bad start in the second half and never could get caught back up," a disappointed Hill-MacDonald observed. "Phoenix played a great series. You have to give them credit."

Even after dropping the series, the Rockers held their heads high. "This is not the end," Michelle Edwards promised after the game-three loss. "This is just the beginning for our team." Although the playoff defeat did not dampen the team's optimism, it did emphasize the Rockers' lack of speed and youthful energy.

Cleveland fans hope that the Rockers' youth movement will begin with such talented youngsters as forward Rushia Brown and guards Adrienne Johnson and Merlakia Jones, who combined for

SUZIE McCONNELL SERIO

more than 20 points per game in 1998. Young guard Cindy Blodgett has also shown potential and appears ready to play a larger role in the team's future.

With increased impact from their younger players, the Rockers should stay a championship contender for years to come. The team's veteran nucleus of Nemcova, Fijalkowski, McConnell Serio, Braxton, and Edwards is among the league's elite, and Coach Hill-MacDonald has proved to be a top strategist and motivator. "Many of the pieces are in place," Hill-MacDonald said. "Now we just have to finish the puzzle."

RESERVES RUSHIA BROWN

(ABOVE) AND ADRIENNE

JOHNSON (BELOW)